The African-in-America:

Connections between African-American HIV/AIDS- Diagnosed Cases & the Incarceration Rate

Jesse Herriott, M.A.

OTHER WORKS BY AUTHOR:

Stop Complaining & Eat Your Pizza: A Mystic's Guide to Meditation, Spirituality, & Family Life

Initiations: Ancient Wisdom for Modern Times

When The Heart Writes: A Collection Of Essays And Articles On The Inner Life

The Book of Neuth: Reflections on the Inner Cosmology of the Soul (coming soon January 2015)

CONTENTS

ACKNOWLEDGMENTS

To my wife and daughter who provided the patience, and space to allow me to complete this two year journey; 2011 would not have been the same without your love and support.

Abstract

The problem of HIV/AIDS in America deserves widespread attention. In fact, minorities make up the majority of HIV/AIDS carriers in the United States. Out of those minorities that are carriers, the group that highest percentage of carriers are African-Americans.

This research utilizes a comparative research methodology to determine and quantify the connection between variables of minority incarceration and minority-diagnosed HIV/AIDS cases. This research also utilizes a meta-analysis of secondary data concerning minority HIV/AIDS cases, and minority incarceration rates to help explain why African-American minorities have some of the highest percentages of cases in both categories. In addition, with a meta-analysis approach, this research utilizes statistical information from secondary data concerning minority HIV/AIDS cases and minority incarceration rates to make these observations, and the secondary data will be obtained from peer-reviewed publications. These sources give insight into relevant peer-reviewed publications and statistical information related to public health, criminal justice, and the incarceration system. This insight is pertinent in order to perform a secondary analysis of research from the periods of the 1960's until the present because it yields the most relevant information related to the subject matter.

Introduction

Background of the Problem

Beginning in the early part of the century, HIV/AIDS was not a widely known disease. Many scholars will suggest that HIV/AIDS has always existed in some capacities, because despite the stigma associated by its name, the effects of this disease have been around for many years. However, these specific affects that are associated with this disease were known by a different name.

This area of research has not seen very much attention in academia, and there have not been huge funded research grants to study some of the causes of HIV infection among African-Americans, along with the highest rates of incarceration by African-Americans as well. One of the interesting notions is that one particular ethnic group is proposed by the majority of research out there, to be at the top of the list in regards to negative things, but they are at the lowest of the list in regards to testing and other measurements (Ledvinka, 1972). As a whole, studies suggest that almost a quarter of a million African Americans have died from AIDS, which is almost half of the percentage of those that died from the disease (Davidson, 2011).

The limitation of this study includes the lack of data in regards to the rate at which prisoners are tested for sexual transmitted diseases after being released back into the population. Also, limitations may include a lack of data concerning the origin, and rate at which people of color originally received transmission of the disease in places around the world and within the U.S.

Statement of the Problem

There is a huge problem with regards to the number of HIV/AIDS cases in the United States and the incarceration rates have much to do with that number. Based on current research, in 2009 over 54,000 Americans as a whole were affected with HIV/AIDS. Out of that number, about 49 percent or more are African-Americans, following by 27% as Caucasian/White, and 21% Hispanic. In the late 90's about 6.3 million people were incarcerated as a whole, (Beckwith, Zaller, Fu, Montague, & Rich, 2010). Out of that population, 17 percent of those that live with the disease were suggested had to have been incarcerated at some time.

Furthermore, vulnerable groups that have been suggested by recent research to be at the highest risk for receiving HIV/AIDS transmission are those that are of the GLBT community, and injecting drug users. Yet, there is no medical evidence that has been produced that suggests if two healthy individuals practice a non-traditional homosexual lifestyle that they will develop HIV/AIDS. However, if one individual, regardless of their sexual preference is undetected, or has any level of the disease in their immune system then they can pass it on to an uninfected person. In addition, there is a vast population of HIV/AIDS based cases where individuals that have been infected while imprisoned, whether certain acts were consensual or not, have contributed to the spread of the disease into the normal population.

There is a strong need for nongovernmental agencies, including but not limited to non-profits, not-for-profits, and even the federal and state government itself to mobilize and take action. In lieu of the current economic situation, this ethical and public health concern is extremely important and it should be intertwined in the public health-care debate. Therefore, the aim of this research to show that educating and raising conscious awareness is a step towards controlling and bringing resolution to this issue.

Literature Review

The purpose of this study is to explore the correlation between HIV/AIDS diagnosed minority cases and the rate of incarceration among minorities. Several key questions that this study will examine are as follows: 1) what is the percentage of minorities that are locked up and have been diagnosed with HIV/AIDS either prior or during their incarceration? and 2) are inmates being properly tested for HIV/AIDS before, during and after being released from incarceration?

History

Many theories exist concerning the origins of the HIV/AIDS virus. Jakob Segal, Wangari Maathai, Alan Cantwell, and others are among those that theorize that the origins of this disease can be traced in a laboratory in America. According to their theories, the HIV/AIDS virus originally occurred in an experiment to combine the viruses Visna and HTLV-1. This virus was then tested on prisoners, which subsequently contributed to the virus' spreading in the normal population (Knight, P., 2003). However, there has not been any scientific evidence from their peers to support their claims. In fact, those that have attempted to speak of the origins of the virus itself have published very little in academic journals. Much of the discussion about the origins of the virus centers around current experiments on the history of particular individuals with the virus. Most of the historical information that is included, briefly mentions initial discovery of the virus to have surfaced during cases in the late 70's.

HIV/AIDS is defined as a progressive loss of the CD4+ helper /inducer subset of "T" cells. When these "T" cells are lost, it damages the immune system, and opens the carrier up to other diseases, infections, and complications of the brain. HIV/AIDS diagnosis among adolescent or adult carriers is based on a drop of the "T" cells below a 200 count, coupled with HIV infection, and one of 25 AIDS indicator conditions (Hutchinson, 2001). However, a person can still fit into the category as a carrier if their "T" cells are up but they still have HIV. If the HIV virus is viewed independently of the AIDS virus, it is treated as a precursor to AIDS. However, medical treatment can be induced to prevent the advancement of the virus from HIV to the more life threatening AIDS virus. Therefore, scientists from many disciplines describe the virus in the form of HIV/AIDS because of their intricate relationship.

Biologists that have endeavored to approach the difficult subject matter suggest that perhaps HIV and AIDS are zoonotic in their origin. Zoonotic viruses can be described as viruses that begin with animals, and they are transferred to people. The Zoonotic origins can be traced to a mutation from the SIV viruses found among primates. SIV is defined as a Simian Immunodeficiency Virus, similar to the way HIV is defined. In many cases the HIV/AIDS virus is thought of to be transmitted only when certain vital fluids are exchanged either in sexual intercourse, blood injections, or during birth (Gilks, 1991). However, what has puzzled Biologists and others from the scientific community about the disease is that earlier outbreaks occurred simultaneously on opposite ends of the globe. In Los Angeles, doctors discovered the degeneration of the immune system in two homosexual men during the initial phases of the disease's appearance. Likewise, in Africa, doctors discovered growths in the pubic and anal regions of women and children (Hooper, 2000).

Biological arguments against the Zoonotic origins of the disease further complicate the discussion of the disease's origins. During the slave trade in the late 1860's, many Africans from the regions of North and West Africa were displaced from their homelands. However, there is a lack of evidence that suggests that when they arrived in the Americas, they brought pathogens and retroviruses with them. Therefore, it cannot be assumed that Africans, who had contact with the animals in their environment, passed along the mutated viruses through modern trade practices (Hooper, 2001). In other words, when the Africans were transported to America, they had contact with animals and it did not result in fatal diseases. Therefore the current HIV/AIDS retrovirus cannot be connected to African interactions with animals, and trade relations today.

Many scholars agree that the infection of the disease

began in Africa, and currently, South Africa serves as the largest

population of HIV/AIDS infected people in the world, making up

over one sixth of the population that are carriers of the disease

(De Cock, 2011). Furthermore, scholars have attempted to explain

the transmission of this disease to the Americas as occurring

because of an increase in innovation, trade, and air transportation.

The rapid increase of air transportation, trade, and commerce

provided a vehicle for carriers to migrate to the Americas

undetected.

All over the globe, and in every country of the world, the

prison population contains the largest percentages of HIV/AIDS

cases in comparison to the general population. In fact, HIV/AIDS

is the second largest explanation for deaths in U.S. prisons.

Furthermore, you are twice as likely to die from HIV/AIDS if you

are incarcerated, (Steinberg, 2005). Subsequently, many

researchers suggest that the United States' response to HIV/AIDS

infection among prisoners lags behind the response to other

countries. Yet, the United States boasts as one of the wealthiest

countries in the world. It was not until the late 90's that states such

as New York, Vermont, Mississippi, Pennsylvania, California, and

Washington D.C. agreed to allow some of their cities to participate in condom distribution programs to try and prevent the spreading of the disease among their prison populations (Steinberg, 2005).

Scholars do not suggest that the cause of infection among the prison population is because countries around the world are discriminating against those that have the disease by arresting them. However, what states are doing is denying the sexual activity and drug usage that occurs in prisons around the world. This alone, can help to explain why a very large portion of the carriers of the disease are incarcerated. Furthermore, minorities, those that are poor, and drug addicts, make up the majority of U.S. prisons (Steinberg, 2005). If those inmates are drug users, or if they are sexually active with other inmates, then their chances for infection are drastically increased.

The correlation between this disease and the carriers in the prison systems bares significant public health concerns. Nicholas Freudenberg suggests that during the early 1980's, the prison systems in New York City housed the largest percentage of HIV/AIDS infected inmates in the country, (Freudenberg, 2011). In addition, correctional facilities have a higher rate, (5.1 percent), of this illness than the normal population. As of 1999, New York

prison systems contained over 7,000 inmates in this situation. If

specific groups within the minority community have the highest

rate of incarceration, and they also make up the highest

percentage of HIV/AIDS carriers, then there is a huge problem in

regards to the transmission of this illness. There appears to be a

serious connection between where the highest rate of the illness is

contained, (prison inmates), and those that make up minority

ethnic groups. Nevertheless, it is very ironic that minority groups

would account for the highest percentage of HIV/AIDS, and also

have the highest incarceration rate.

Minority Incarceration

According to Dr. Nacona Peterson, there are over

2 million people incarcerated in the United States, and the

U.S. has one of the largest numbers of citizens that are

imprisoned in the world, (Peterson, & Severson, 2003).

Out of that figure that Dr. Peterson suggests, it could be

safe to presume that about forty percent would constitute

African-Americans, followed by Latinos, and other

minorities. Coupled with a high percentage of HIV/AIDS

diagnosed cases, it could appear that the minority community is exhibiting some action, or some form of behavior that non-minorities are not exhibiting. However, that is not the case, and according to Peterson, minorities are affected the greatest in regards to issues of public health, and incarceration because of "white privilege", (Peterson, & Severson, 2003).

So then, what is the concept of "white privilege" and how does it relate to the public health concerns and legal concerns of other ethnic groups in America? Well, in this case, the author would be suggesting that criminal activity for certain ethnic groups are overlooked. If that is that case, then the legal system would definitely have an alternate set of rules that only apply based on your skin complexion. Indeed there are disparities as it pertains to treatment of suspect classes in America. However, the problem with the huge incarceration of minorities and our statistics that 1 out of every 100 adult being incarcerated far exceeds the cries of racism. The real problem is with public policy.

HIV/AIDS and Incarceration

HIV/AIDS carriers that were infected with the disease either prior or during their incarceration are high, particularly for minorities. From the research that is available, about 65 percent of state prison inmates where either racial or ethnic minorities in 1991, which is up from 60 percent in the late 1980's. Out of that population it is estimated that about half of them are Black or of African American ethnicity, 20 percent are Hispanic, 1 percent are Asian, 36 percent are white, and 0 percent are Native-American, (Beckwith, Zaller, Fu, Montague, & Rich, 2010).

Among women, fifty-six percent of those with HIV/AIDS are African-American. In fact, some statistics even suggest that well over 22,480 as a whole are infected with the disease are incarcerated, making HIV/AIDS about four times as common among inmates than the general population. Based on that research, it can be hypothesized that there is a striking correlation between those that have served time within the prison systems, and the percentage of HIV/AIDS cases, especially those among minority women. Those that are released back into the population do not necessarily have the same level of health care afforded to them in the prisons. Also, coupled with the guilt or shame of knowing they may have received this disease, in some cases through traumatic events, they may hide the disease and pass it on to unsuspecting partners, thus contributing to the percentage of citizens that are diagnosed with the disease.

In the early 90's, over 600,000 inmates were released from either prison or jail. Research suggests that the majority of inmates were minorities, poor, or drug users (Steinberg, 2005). Therefore, they probably matriculated back into the areas and neighborhoods where they originated from. Consequently, those that were of the general public may not have been notified that their friends, loved ones, or relatives were infected with the disease. In fact, at least 17 percent of the general population in the late 90's was incarcerated at some time (Steinberg, 2005). Seventeen percent is not a small number when considering the amount of people that lived in America during that time. Therefore, through various means, the disease slowly spread throughout the population, drastically affecting the general population that are minorities, drug users, and those that are poor.

Sexual activity in Prisons

In a previous study regarding the sexual activity among inmates in male maximum security prison, the researchers' goal was to modify some of the myths that have been associated with prisoner behavior. In their study, the researchers suggest that out of the subjects that were surveyed about their sexual disposition, and activity, over eighty percent of the participants classified themselves as heterosexual, (Hensley, Tewksbury, & Wright, 2001). In other words, despite the statistics, there is also a portion of those that are incarcerated that do not identify themselves with the behavior that would otherwise place them in the path of possibly becoming infected or contaminated with a sexually transmitted disease while they are incarcerated. Furthermore, out of those subjects that were surveyed, ninety-nine percent of those that are incarcerated suggest that they relieve their hormonic tensions own their own.

However, a closer look at the study of the researchers suggest that although there is some validity to the inmates' story, there is also the possibility that perhaps the inmates will not disclose other forms of behavior that may seem contrary to the norm because it contradicts their pre-incarcerated identities, or their religious affiliation. Out of the 99% that suggested that they relieved themselves on their own, almost half of that population admitted to participating in some form of intimate behavior with other inmates while incarcerated, (Hensley, Tewksbury, & Wright, 2001).

Research from the University of Mexico suggests that injection drug users, (IDU's) run the risk of becoming infected with the HIV/AIDS. According to Dr. Estrada, who was the lead investigator in regards to this issue, HIV has taken on a since of normalcy for those that inject drugs. Also, Dr. Estrada's research promotes "the possibility of receiving and transmitting this illness ranges between fifty to ninety percent", (Estrada, 2007). Nevertheless, a study produced by Routledge University indicates that in order to fully engage this predicament that a more holistic program would need to be designed that accounted for other areas that could contribute to the rise of HIV/AIDS among minorities other than drugs. These areas are inclusive of the following: abuse, coercion, sexual identity, dating issues, and intimacy issues, (Seal, Kelly, Bloom, Stevenson, Coley, & Broyles, 2000).

HIV/AIDS Prison Care

Additionally, inmates are not properly tested for HIV/AIDS before, during and after being released from incarceration. According to recent research, since 2006, about 21 states are implementing some type of procedure for testing prior to or during incarcerations. Of those procedures, the categories that they fall into are compulsory testing, optional testing, and no testing, (Duffus, Youmans, Gibson, & Albrecht, 2009). The first method is where the inmates are forced to screen for the disease. The second method is where the testing is offered to them and the prisoners can choose whether or not to be screened. The last method is where they are only tested if individually an inmate asks to be tested. In regards to testing upon release, according to the center for disease control, inmates must at least be given the option to test but it is not mandatory.

Furthermore, some of the methods that HIV/AIDS is

transmitted in prisons is by way of either consensual or forced sexual relations, injecting drug usage, or tattooing which pierces the various layers of skin. In particular, for the drug usage problem, since it is illegal to use drugs, the needles that are used to inject drugs will have a high probability of being shared and passed around since it would be difficult to clean needles. Based on the research that is available, it can be hypothesized that among the populations in various countries around the world that HIV or AIDS is a person-person transmittable disease.

In short, it can be suggested that one single individual cannot develop the disease on their own and then pass it to someone; they would have to have received a transmission of it from a carrier. Factors that contribute to the rate of HIV/AIDS among African-Americans in prison and African-Americans in the normal population have been suggested as being directly correlated with severe socio-economic circumstances, promiscuity, lack of education, unhealthy ecosystems, and poor health care. In fact, African-American women are suggested to have the highest risk of HIV/AIDS infection as a result of intimate heterosexual relationships,

(Ferguson, Y., Quinn, S., Eng, E. E., & Sandelowski,

2006).

The goal of this research is to promote public health and increase the consciousness and awareness of not just the academic community, but also for the general public about the rate of transmission of this disease; not to mention the pending health care argument in connection with medical coverage for carriers. Furthermore, this study carries an interdisciplinary approach as it explores some of the treatment of former convicts and examines their connection to this plight, as well as the policy argument around whether or not they are properly tested for sexual-transmitted-diseases before, during, and after release back into the general population.

Prison Guard Rape

The sexual activity of prisoners in America is a subject that is not discussed in public domain. The majority of prisoner's will confirm that if there is any activity of sexual nature that occurs, it is mostly through self-pleasure. However, that testimony would not be able to account for reports of prisoner abuse which happens under some circumstances by prison guards, and by other inmates. Proving that abuse occurred from intentional acts by the prison guards that were on watch would be difficult for any inmate, due to the past conviction that placed them in custody in the first place (Moster & Jeglic, 2009). Furthermore, out of the half a million prisoners that are discharged annually, if there is a large percentage of those former inmates that were raped, it could impair their ability to "fit" back into society. As a result, they may return back to a life of crime, which would only add to the already high recidivism rate in America, (Eckholm, 2008).

The deliberate indifference clause would be difficult for a prisoner to prove, if they were assaulted by a prison guard. In fact, this clause, which is part of a test that requires prisoners to show that their circumstances cause them to be in danger, would be difficult to prove for anyone that has ever been abused. Coupled with that piece of the test is an additional requirement where prisoners would have to show the negligence of other prison guards in preventing the incident as well (Male Rape, 2001). However, female rape in prisons maybe easier to prove, only because of the added risk of becoming pregnant while incarcerated would raise a red flag with prison administration.

In America, the female prison population is dominated by African-American females, with Latino females following behind as the next largest ethnic group in women prisons (Jordon-Zachery, 2004). When you couple the problem with prison rape along with the percentage of male guards that are staffed in female prisons, it appears problematic that males are overstaffed in female prisons (Buchanon, 2005). Female prison guards can perform with the same intelligence and professionalism that male prison guards can. In fact, recent studies suggest that female prison guards are taken just as serious as male prison guards (Boyd & Grant, 2005).

Profiling based on Gender

Profiling based on sexuality is a popular discussion in the media and in today's culture. Many states are beginning policy reform in light of this new wave of activism. Those in the law enforcement community have been cited for unfair approaches in their sting operations, in which unfair arrests of those within the LGBT community have been cited, (Hauser & Mascia, 2009). What becomes an interesting question is one that involves the amount of discretion that police officers have. Police should have a certain amount of discretion when they are attempting to prevent criminal

activity. However profiling based on sexuality is serious problem

when the majority of the law enforcement in today's culture is

dominated by Caucasian males (Myers, Forest, & Miller, 2004).

Research Methodology

The purpose of this study was to provide a thorough
examination for both the academic and the public alike, of
previous and recent research on the vast percentage of
HIV/AIDS cases among minorities. In addition, this
research seeks to discover if a connection exists between
that research and the rate of incarceration among
minorities within the U.S, and also to clarify what that
connection is. Furthermore, this study attempted to
discover other alternative explanations for minority's
diagnosis of HIV/AIDS.

A meta-analysis research design was chosen as the appropriate methodological approach in consideration of the availability of data, and constraint of time and the budget necessary to complete this research. A meta-analysis will allow this research to statistically analyze and integrate the conclusions of a multitude of studies that reference the similar subjects of inquiry, (Glass, 1976). Furthermore, this particular approach will allow this research to use statistical programs such as SPSS to investigate the features and outcomes of the current research, (Glass, 1976). This research will complete this process by accurately describing problematic areas, and investigating relevant literature from previous studies. Also, this research will construct a specific metric or data-set in order to analyze the information and to accurately provide a conclusion of the results.

The current study utilized seven variables in order to examine if there was a connection between minority incarceration rates and diagnosed cases of minorities with HIV/AIDS. This method was chosen in order to complete the project with the secondary source material that was available. In that regards, the seven variables that were used in the current study were used and compared across the chosen studies were: Ethnicity (which was divided into the three categories of Black/White & Latino), Sample (which was the total number of inmates that participated in the chosen study), Author (the author of the selected population study), Infection (whether or not the population sample where infected with HIV/AIDS), and State (which was the state prison the inmate population was selected from). The infection category was entered in then given a simple yes or no answer as to whether or not the specified population sample were diagnosed with the HIV/AIDS virus. If it was mentioned in the study as a strong predictor that a specific group were diagnosed with the virus, then they were given a yes.

In order to access as much pertinent information as possible for the research at hand, a keyword search was performed, utilizing the keywords *HIV-AIDS and African-Americans, prison rape, HIV-AIDS and incarceration, and African-American incarceration.* This procedure was carried out through the usage of Keiser University's

Library database, EBSCO host database, SIRS Knowledge Source database. Specifically, these databases contain thousands of peer-reviewed publications that are uploaded on a very consistent basis. These resources have a wide variety of scholarly publications, including those that are relevant to the current research such as controversial issues in the legal system, criminal justice, public health, corrections, and even pieces from other publications.

This research undertaking utilized specific variables in order to remain on task with the chosen topic. The statistical software that will be used to complete the analysis of this research will be IBM's SPSS 19 software, which is acquirable for Keiser University's MACJ students. This software allows the researcher to test and   analyze, data that is gathered so that the outcomes can be reviewed and interpreted.

Incarcerated / community correction – This portion of the study included participant data from a corrections facility. The mixed male/female sample size for this study is 2,699 participants.

The sample size included an analysis of inmates in adult male prisons only.

Description of the Results

Three statistical tests were run on the collected data:
a frequencies test, cross-tabulations, and a Oneway
ANOVA. The data collected was re-analyzed using
secondary data Frequency analysis is a descriptive
statistical method that shows the number of times a given
response was chosen by respondents. Tables were
incorporated which show variables that yield percentages
and numerical values based on the number of participants
that responded to a specific inquiry during the study
(Carver & Nash, 2009). Cross-tabulation is used to
compare the relationship between two variables in a

study.

What the data shows in table 1.1 is that whether or not the selected inmates that were currently incarcerated were positive for HIV or the AIDS virus. Based on a comparison of primary source data from the selected studies of Baillargeon (2010), Stephens (2004), and Valera (2009), there was a higher percentage of inmates that were not affected with HIV prior to incarceration, or during incarceration. The data can be viewed as indicating that the majority of the participants in the study did not admit that they were positive for HIV or AIDS. Also, based on a cross-tabulation of the data, out of the state prison systems that the incarcerated participants were selected from, only one out of the three states yielded inmates that were actually positive of the HIV/AIDS virus while they were currently incarcerated (table 2.1). This is interesting because the results suggest that either Texas state prison systems has a higher rate of HIV/AIDS inmates, or their inmates were more likely to cooperate with the study. In addition, the data in table 2.2 and 2.3, the information suggests that out of the total population of participants, Blacks have the highest rate of HIV/AIDS, followed by Whites and then Latinos.

Whether or not the selected participants were HIV positive				
	Frequency	Percent	Valid Percent	Cumulative Percent
Valid	7	70.0	70.0	70.0
No	2	20.0	20.0	90.0
Yes	1	10.0	10.0	100.0
Total	10	100.0	100.0	

(Table 1.1) The Frequency rates higher of those admitting in the studies to have

the HIV/AIDS virus.

State the Sample took place in * Whether or not the selected participants were HIV positive Cross-tabulation

Count

	Whether or not the selected participants were HIV positive			Total
		No	Yes	
State the Sample took place in	7	0	0	7
Georgia	0	1	0	1
New York	0	1	0	1

Texas	0	0	1	1
Total	7	2	1	10

(Table 2.1) The Frequency rates higher for Texas inmates who have HIV/AIDS.

State the Sample took place in * Black inmates Cross-tabulation

Count

State the Sample took place in	Black inmates			Total
	160	314	1241	
Georgia	1	0	0	1
New York	0	1	0	1
Texas	0	0	1	1
Total	1	1	1	3

(Table 2.2) The Frequency rates higher of those that were Black in the studies

and have the HIV/AIDS virus.

Number incarcerated participants for this specific study * Black inmates Cross-tabulation

Count

		Latinos	Whites	Blacks	Total
		229	447	1241	
Number of incarcerated participants for this specific study	1917	0	0	0	0
Total	1917	0	0	0	1

(Table 2.3) The total number of participants in the three studies suggests that Black inmates have the highest rates for HIV/AIDS virus.

The ANOVA procedure, or Analysis of Variance, is used to test theories about means whenever there are various samples of the populations. Also, the ANOVA procedure is used to determine if they are equal, (Carver & Nash, 2009). This study shows that among Blacks, there is a 341934.333 mean square difference between the two sets of groups when compared to other ethnicities that were sampled in the study.

ANOVA

		Sum of Squares	df	Mean Square
Black inmates	Between Groups	683868.667	2	341934.333
	Within Groups	.000	0	.
	Total	683868.667	2	

White inmates	Between Groups	107004.667	2	53502.333
	Within Groups	.000	0	.
	Total	107004.667	2	
Latino inmates	Between Groups	28740.667	2	14370.333
	Within Groups	.000	0	.
	Total	28740.667	2	

(Table 3.1) Blacks have a higher mean square difference of 341934.333 in the

two sets of groups.

Summary

The purpose of this study was to explore the correlation between HIV/AIDS diagnosed minority cases and the rate of incarceration among minorities. By identifying if a correlation exists, it will contribute to the growing body of research regarding public health and public policy concerns within minority communities. In fact, initiatives that can provide funding for more research, or better education and healthcare will have more success in solving this issue than any other approach to combat this problem. Those that are within the communities that have been infected cannot be forced to receive help. However, if the information is presented, they will have the opportunity to make that choice; as opposed to isolating themselves because there aren't any solutions available. Research shows that among the inmates that were selected for the mentioned studies, there was only a small amount of inmates or former inmates that actually admitted their HIV/AIDS status. It is within the inmates rights to maintain their privacy. Yet, when compared to the large percentages of inmates that have tested positive for the disease, it is evident that they do need help.

Conclusions

In regards to limitations of the current study, more data will have to be collected. Primary source information will have to be obtained, and researchers will need the cooperation of various prison wardens, health review boards, and policy experts. In the current study, only one state prison, (Texas), yielded the greatest amount of participation. In addition, researchers should perform more tests to determine if more inmates are being affected at a greater capacity during prison. Also, researchers should study to find out if inmates are bringing the disease with them when they become incarcerated. In fact, some studies suggest that at least twenty percent of inmates with HIV/AIDS that are released, return back to prison within 3 years of being released (Baillargeon, Giordano, Harzke, Spaulding, Wu, Grady, & Paar, 2010). This would be a substantial amount of time to spread the virus, if the former inmates do not receive the same level of health care after being released, which they received while incarcerated.

Further limitations of the current study include the minimal amount of sample data and studies that was available. Also, a portion of this investigation suggests that there is a desperate need for more research on the specific correlations between African-American incarceration rates and African-American diagnoses of HIV/AIDS. This is very vital to future endeavors that use both primary and secondary sources because if a realistic problem can be found, then a solution can be developed. Most importantly, negative stereotypes about African-Americans and minorities in general will be quieted because they will not have the highest percentages in everything negative in America.

A more specific recommendation for future

researchers would be to develop a theory and assessment tool that helps to analyze the statistical data that they receive. Sometimes statistical data can be a bit ambiguous, and may only serve the will of the researcher. In many cases, the answer to the biggest problem can come from the simplest solution. In that light, solutions as well as data will have to be simplified for the general public, as well as various organizations that may want to contribute to solving this problem. This problem should be approached from an interdisciplinary angle because it encompasses aspects of public health, medical, education, legal, public policy, and criminological disciplines.

References

Baillargeon, J., Giordano, T. P., Harzke, A.,
Spaulding, A. C., Wu, Z., Grady, J. J., & ... Paar, D.
P. (2010). Predictors of Incarceration and Disease
Progression Among Released HIV-Infected Inmates.
AIDS Patient Care & STDs, 24(6), 389-394.
doi:10.1089/apc.2009.0303

Beckwith, C. G., Zaller, N. D., Fu, J. J., Montague, B. T., &
Rich, J. D. (2010). Opportunities to Diagnose, Treat, and
Prevent HIV in the Criminal Justice System. *JAIDS:*
Journal of Acquired Immune Deficiency Syndromes,
55S49-S55. Retrieved from EBSCO*host*.

Carver, R., Nash, J. (2009). Doing Data Analysis with
SPSS: Belmont, CA: Cengage Learning.

Davidson, L.(2011). African Americans and HIV/AIDS-The
Epidemic Continues: An Intervention to Address the
HIV/AIDS Pandemic in the Black Community. *Journal of*
Black   Studies,   42(1),   83-105.
Doi:10.1177/0021934710367902.

De Cock, K. M., Jaffe, H. W., & Curran, J. W. (2011). Reflections on 30 Years of AIDS. Emerging Infectious Diseases, 17(6), 1044-1048. doi:10.3201/eid1706.100184

Duffus, W. A., Youmans, E., Stephens, T., Gibson, J. J., Albrecht, H., & Potter, R. H. (2009). Missed Opportunities for Early HIV Diagnosis in Correctional Facilities. *AIDS Patient Care & STDs*, 23(12), 1025-1032. doi:10.1089/apc.2009.0197

Estrada, A. (2007). HIV and HCV Infection among Minority Drug Injectors. *FASEB Journal*, 21(5), A149. Retrieved from EBSCO *host*.

Ferguson, Y., Quinn, S., Eng, E. E., & Sandelowski, M. M. (2006). The gender ratio imbalance and its relationship to risk of HIV/AIDS among African American women at historically black colleges and universities. AIDS Care, 18(4), 323-331.

Freudenberg, N. (2011). HIV in the Epicenter of the Epicenter: HIV and Drug Use Among Criminal Justice Populations in New York City, 1980--2007. *Substance*

Use & Misuse, 46(2/3), 159-170. doi:10.3109/10826084.2011.521460

Gilks C. (1991). AIDS, Monkeys and Malaria. *Nature* 354:262.

Gough, E., Kempf, M. C., Graham, L., Manzanero, M., Hook, E. W., Bartolucci, A., & Chamot, E. (2010). HIV and Hepatitis B and C incidence rates in US correctional populations and high risk groups: a systematic review and meta-analysis. *BMC Public Health*, 10777-790. doi:10.1186/1471-2458-10-777

Glass, G. (1976). Primary, secondary and meta-analysis of research. Educational Researcher,

5, 3-8.

Hensley, C., Tewksbury, R., & Wright, J. (2001). Exploring the Dynamics of Masturbation and Consensual Same-Sex Activity Within a Male Maximum Security Prison. Journal of Men's Studies, 10(1), 59-71. Retrieved from EBSCO host.

Hooper, E. E. (2000). How did AIDS Get Started?. South

African Journal of Science, 96(6), 265. Retrieved from EBSCOhost.

Hutchinson, J. (2001). THE BIOLOGY AND EVOLUTION OF HIV. Annual Review of Anthropology, 30(1), 85. Retrieved from EBSCOhost.

Khan, M. R., Behrend, L., Adimora, A. A., Weir, S. S., White, B. L., & Wohl, D. A. (2011). Dissolution of Primary Intimate Relationships during Incarceration and Implications for Post-release HIV Transmission. *Journal of Urban Health*, 88(2), 365-375. doi:10.1007/s11524-010-9538-1

Knight, P. (2003). Conspiracy Theories in America. ABC-CLIO: Santa Barbara, California.

Ledvinka, J. (1972). The Intrusion of Race: Black Responses to the White Observer. *Social Science Quarterly (Southwestern Social Sciences Association)*, 52(4), 907-920. Retrieved from EBSCO *host*.

Pewewardy, N., & Severson, M. (2003). A Threat to Liberty: White Privilege and Disproportionate Minority incarceration. *Journal of Progressive Human Services*, 14(2), 53-74. Retrieved from EBSCO *host*.

Rosen, D. L., Schoenbach, V. J., Wohl, D. A., White, B. L., Stewart, P. W., & Golin, C. E. (2009). An Evaluation of HIV Testing Among Inmates in the North Carolina Prison System. *American Journal of Public Health*, 99(S2), S452-S459. Retrieved from EBSCO *host*.

Seal, D. W., Kelly, J. A., Bloom, F. R., Stevenson, L. Y., Coley, B. I., & Broyles, L. A. (2000). HIV prevention with young men who have sex with men: what young men themselves say is needed. *AIDS Care*, 12(1), 5-26. doi:10.1080/09540120047431

Spaulding, A. C., Seals, R. M., McCallum, V. A., Perez, S. D., Brzozowski, A. K., & Steenland, N. (2011). Prisoner Survival Inside and Outside of the Institution: Implications for Health-Care Planning. *American Journal of Epidemiology*, 173(5), 479-487. doi:10.1093/aje/kwq422

Steinberg, R. G. (2005). Unprotected: HIV Prison Policy and the Deadly Politics of Denial. Harvard Journal of

African American Public Policy, 1143-49. Retrieved from EBSCOhost.

Stephens, T., Braithwaite, R., & Tiggs, C. (2004). Correlates of inmates' self-reported HIV/AIDS risk behaviors, prior incarceration, and marijuana use. The American Journal Of Drug And Alcohol Abuse, 30(2), 287-298. Retrieved from EBSCO host.

Eckholm, E. (2008, April 8). U.S. Shifting Prison Focus To Re-entry Into Society. New York Times. p. 23. Retrieved from EBSCO host..

Myers, K. A., Forest, K. B., & Miller, S. L. (2004). Officer Friendly and the Tough Cop: Gays and Lesbians Navigate Homophobia and Policing. Journal of Homosexuality, 47(1), 17-37. Retrieved from EBSCO host.

Hauser, C. & Mascia, J. (2009). Among Gay Men, Arrests Spark Concern About Being Singled Out. New York Times. p.33. Retrieved from EBSCO host.

Buchanan, K. (2005). Beyond Modesty: Privacy in Prison and the Risk of Sexual Abuse: Marquette Law Review, 88(4), 751-813.

Retrieved from EBSCO *host.*

Boyd, E., & Grant, T. (2005). Is gender a factor in perceived prison officer competence? Male prisoners' perceptions in an English dispersal prison. Criminal Behavior & Mental Health, 15(1), 65-74. Retrieved from EBSCO host.

Jordon-Zachery, J. S. (2004). The Other Prison Population: Black Women and the Prison Industrial Complex. Conference Papers -- Western Political Science Association, 1-20. doi:wpsa_proceeding_12866.PDF

Report: Male rape victims in prison get little empathy. (2001). Contemporary Sexuality, 35(5), 8. Retrieved from EBSCO host.

Moster, A. N., & Jeglic, E. L. (2009). Prison Warden Attitudes Toward Prison Rape and Sexual Assault: Findings Since the Prison Rape Elimination Act (PREA). Prison Journal, 89(1), 65-78. doi:10.1177/0032885508329981

Valera, P., Epperson, M., Daniels, J., Ramaswamy, M., & Freudenberg, N. (2009). Substance use and HIV-risk behaviors among young men involved in the criminal justice system. The American Journal Of Drug And Alcohol Abuse, 35(1), 43-47.

Retrieved from EBSCO host

About the Author

Jesse Herriott is a Writer, Teacher, & Spiritual Researcher whose work explores what it means to be human. He is an ordained priest in the Universal Anglican Church and a senior "Acharya" in the RHIMES tradition of interspirituality. Jesse has Bachelor and Master degrees in Criminal Justice and Political Science from both the Univ. of S.C. and Keiser University respectively, and an honorary Doctor of Ministry degree from Anglican Divinity School. And he lectures frequently within churches, spiritual centers, and career colleges throughout the state of Georgia. His writings can be found on unity.org, elephant journal magazine, and a host of other online publications. His radio show "Living on Purpose" is archived on Unity Online Radio at: www.unity.fm/program/livingonpurpose and his website is www.jessherriott.com. His newest podcast project, "Heart and Soul Radio" is updated weekly on his website, and other social media channels. Jesse's latest endeavor involves distilling his work into what he calls, "The Path" which is an in-depth exploration of ways in which we can live from our hearts and be deeply connected to our souls. He is the author of: *Stop Complaining & Eat Your Pizza: A Mystic's Guide to Meditation, Spirituality,*

& Family Life

Initiations: Ancient Wisdom for Modern Times

When The Heart Writes: A Collection Of Essays And Articles On The Inner Life

The Book of Neuth: Reflections on the Inner Cosmology of the Soul (coming soon January 2015)